My N Words

Consultants

Ashley Bishop, Ed.D.
Sue Bishop, M.E.D.

Publishing Credits

Dona Herweck Rice, *Editor-in-Chief*

Robin Erickson, *Production Director*

Lee Aucoin, *Creative Director*

Sharon Coan, *Project Manager*

Jamey Acosta, *Editor*

Rachelle Cracchiolo, M.A.Ed., *Publisher*

Image Credits

cover Roman Sigaev/Shutterstock; p.2 Kuhan/Shutterstock; p.3 mihalec/Shutterstock; p.4 Rob Stark/Shutterstock; p.5 Roman Sigaev/Shutterstock; p.6 Serhiy Shullye/Shutterstock; p.7 CLM/Shutterstock; p.8 Bayanova Svetlana/Shutterstock.com; p.9 dedek/Shutterstock; p.10 Roman Sigaev/Shutterstock; back cover Roman Sigaev/Shutterstock

Teacher Created Materials

5301 Oceanus Drive
Huntington Beach, CA 92649-1030
http://www.tcmpub.com
ISBN 978-1-4333-2556-4
© 2012 Teacher Created Materials, Inc.

I see a **n**urse.

I see a **n**ail.

I see a **nut**.

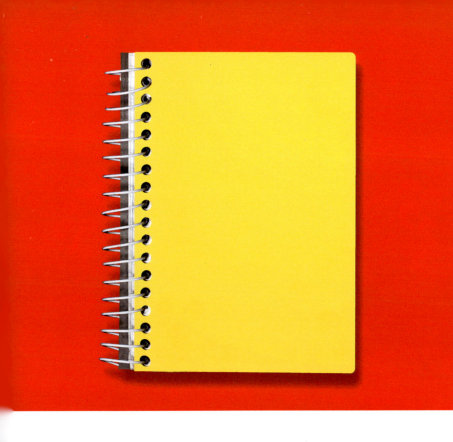

I see a **n**otebook.

I see a necklace

I see a **n**eedle.

I see a **n**apkin.

I see a **n**et.

I see a **n**est.

Glossary

Sight Words

I　see　a

Activities

- Read the book aloud to your child, pointing to the *n* words as you say them. After reading each page, ask, "What do you see?"

- Go to a craft store for materials so that your child can make a beaded necklace. Encourage him or her to be creative by using different colors or patterns. Remind him or her that the word *necklace* begins with *n*.

- Talk with your child about birds and how they build their nests.

- Go to the library and find a picture book about nurses. Read it with your child and talk about how sometimes nurses give us shots with needles to make sure we stay healthy.

- Help your child think of a personally valuable word to represent the letter *n*, such as *nice*.